Crime Detection and
Prevention Series
Paper 74

Policing Problem Housing Estates

Sheridan Morris

Editor: Barry Webb
Home Office
Police Research Group
50 Queen Anne's Gate
London SW1H 9AT

Police Research Group: Crime Detection and Prevention Series

The Home Office Police Research Group (PRG) was formed in 1992 to carry out and manage research relevant to the work of the police service. The terms of reference for the Group include the requirement to identify and disseminate good practice to the police.

The Crime Detection and Prevention Series follows on from the Crime Prevention Unit papers, a series which has been published by the Home Office since 1983. The recognition that effective crime strategies will often involve both crime prevention and crime investigation, however, has led to the scope of this series being broadened. This new series will present research material on both crime prevention and detection in a way which informs policy and practice throughout the service.

A parallel series of papers on resource management and organisational issues is also published by PRG, as is a periodical on policing research called 'Focus'.

ISBN 1-85893-656-X

Foreword

Some housing estates present particular difficulties to the police, not just because of the concentration of crime on them but also the more general problem of anti-social behaviour which can make significant demand on police resources. This report identifies policing strategies which have helped 'turn around' a number of such estates.

The policing strategies identified here have included various forms of high profile policing operations together with a more 'problem oriented policing' approach, an approach which seeks solutions to problems of crime and nuisance rather than continues to respond to them in a conventional way. The co-ordination of police and local authority activity to support the use of civil legislation emerges as a particular and increasingly used solution to some of these problems on housing estates. Work supported by PRG is currently underway in Leicestershire Constabulary to explore the potential for more routine adoption of problem oriented policing in Britain.

S W BOYS SMITH
Director of Police Policy
Home Office
June 1996

Acknowledgements

I wish to express my gratitude to the police officers and local authority staff in all the areas visited, including those which were not fully used in this report. All gave freely of their time and afforded the author generous assistance and access to relevant material

Sheridan Morris
June 1996

The Author

The author is a member of the Home Office Police Research Group.

PRG would like to thank Professor Mike Maguire of the School of Administrative and Social Studies at the University of Wales College of Cardiff for acting as external assessor for this report.

Executive summary

Background

Every police force will have at least one estate or residential area which represents a hotspot, either in terms of a high volume of incidents or as a potential public order problem. A survey of local authorities found that between 10 and 40% of respondents' housing stock was affected with "crime such as to interfere with the lives of tenants". A lot of research has examined how such problems can be tackled, leading to numerous and diverse initiatives.

This report set out to identify effective practices in policing problem residential areas. The 43 forces in England and Wales were approached for suitable examples. Of the thirty that put forward potential candidates, six have been examined in depth and documented here as providing lessons for more widespread adoption.

Recommendations

This report recommends action on three broad fronts to tackle the numerous and varying problems posed by problem housing estates.

Police enforcement

Key offenders should be dealt with through the collection and use of intelligence and targeted operations. Particular problems may be suitable for high profile targeted patrolling by dedicated units or personnel. Such intervention must be directed and clearly explained to local residents. Less entrenched offending can be disrupted by 'pulse policing' techniques and maximising the police presence.

Civil enforcement

The civil nature of many incidents should be addressed by the use of civil law, such as evictions and injunctions. The police should, where practicable, encourage and facilitate such actions by the local authority. Police support can be given by providing information and reporting injunction breaches.

Community investment

Long term solutions will require the support of the community. Residents must be engaged by local officers who should be encouraged and supported in taking a longer term problem oriented approach to incidents. Prejudices must be worn down through non-confrontational contract and the young must be exposed to a positive police presence before negative attitudes regarding the police become ingrained. The perceptions of residents and rumour control must be given a greater priority. The media should be seen as a resource not a threat and used accordingly.

Strategy

All three approaches should be used strategically, with both short and long term measures combined to maximise the effectiveness of the strategy. The specific balance between the three approaches will vary with the problems faced and over time.

Contents

List of Tables

List of Figures

1. Introduction

Problem estates

Many police commanders are likely to have within their area an estate which presents them with particular policing difficulties. The 1992 British Crime Survey indicated that residents of the poorest council estates in inner city or outer conurbation locations (ACORN G: council estates category III) experienced almost three times the national average risk of burglary and attempted burglary. Less well off council estates (ACORN F: council estates category II) experience one and a half times the national average for actual and attempted burglaries. Mixed inner city areas (ACORN H: multi-racial, low-income and made up of private rental, owner occupiers and council tenants) suffer almost double the average incidence of burglary (Mayhew et al, 1992). All three categories experience higher than average levels of vehicle crime.

Such estates have achieved a reputation for potential public disorder incidents. Two case studies (Toxteth and the Meadow Well) in this report achieved national notoriety following serious disorders in 1981 and 1991. The Meadow Well disturbance occurred around the same time as large scale disorder on estates in Cardiff, Oxford and the Newcastle area. Various triggers have been put forward for such disturbances but common themes are invariably high levels of socio-economic deprivation stemming from unemployment, often accompanied by poor police-community relations.

More recently, a survey by the Association of Metropolitan Authorities found that respondents indicated that between 10 and 40% of their housing stock was affected with 'crime such as to interfere with the lives of tenants' (AMA, 1994). The same authorities each identified an average of approximately eight estate areas where crime was a definable problem affecting the lives of residents.

Criminal and public order incidents are but one indicator of the 'problematic' nature of living in such estates and a body of literature and initiatives has developed around what is termed 'incivilities', 'anti-social' or 'nuisance' behaviour. Such behaviours may include excessive noise by residents, intimidation by groups of youths and harassment by neighbours. Such incidents are frequently of a civil rather than criminal nature, giving the police little basis on which to intervene effectively.

Tackling the problems

The Department of the Environment (1993) allocates estate and area improvement initiatives to five categories:

Design changes. Building predominantly on the work of Newman (1972) and his successors, this has often taken the form of 'creative demolition' and is seen in the partial re-designing and rebuilding of many large estate developments.

Management changes. An approach which is essentially based upon the devolvement of estate management, often to an on-site office with devolved control and responsibility for local services, such as maintenance and neighbour disputes. Tenant participation is often encouraged, for example in the Priority Estates Project (PEP) scheme and currently, the creation of local Housing Action Trusts (HATs).

Security measures. These include the installation of intercom systems, concierges, CCTV and improved security of doors and windows.

Social measures. An approach aimed at actual and potential offenders. Local schemes can take the form of youth diversion schemes and support services provided in local community centres.

Policing measures. Various police tactics have been tried to manage 'hot spots' effectively, either in terms of potential public order threats or a high level of incident calls. Tactics vary from Community Beat Officers and problem oriented policing, to high profile crackdowns.

The research

This research is aimed at identifying effective policing strategies for dealing with problem housing estates. It therefore focuses on predominantly policing and other enforcement measures. A broader overview of the area is provided in 'Crime Prevention on Housing Estates' by the Department of the Environment (1993).

Identifying the estates

Estates were examined which had formerly been 'problematic' to police, but had apparently experienced a 'turnaround' as a result of police, and often multi-agency, intervention. All 43 forces in England and Wales were surveyed by telephone and asked whether the force had any 'success stories' which would be suitable as a potential case study. Of the 43 forces approached, 13 indicated that they had nothing suitable. Details were taken from officers in the remaining 30 forces. On the basis of the information gained from the phone survey and material provided by forces and local authorities, an initial shortlist of nine estates was drawn up. These were visited and meetings held with police and relevant local authority and agency officers. As stated previously, the project concentrated on initiatives which were predominantly based around innovative police operations, rather than wider multi-agency partnerships or previously documented police schemes.

Four estates were chosen for study in full, and imaginative police initiatives described in two others. Varying in type and presenting differing problems, the estates examined were:

- Toxteth, Liverpool

- Broxtowe Estate, Nottingham

- Kingsmead Estate, London

- Gateshead, Newcastle (police initiative only)

- Meadow Well Estate, North Shields

- Killingbeck, Leeds (police initiative only)

These case studies are presented in Section 2 of the report. Evaluating the selected sites involved detailing the initiatives undertaken and examining recorded crime and other available information (eg. void rates, the number of vacant properties) to find evidence of any improvement. The limitations of such indicators, along with anecdotal evidence, is acknowledged, but is considered sufficient to allow the extrapolation of practices and principles to be put forward in section 3, for local commanders to examine and implement according to their own judgement and local conditions.

2. The case studies

Toxteth, Liverpool

This case study illustrates the application of two diverse but complementary strategies, a vigorous 'street' enforcement policy and a long term investment in youth and community relations. This study will examine the period 1993-1994.

Toxteth is a large residential area (though not an estate as such) in south west Liverpool, which achieved national notoriety following major public disorder incidents in 1981. Almost half the property is terraced housing, another 20% comprising of flats. Forty percent of households are council tenants and 15% owner occupied.

The major focus of criminality in Toxteth is an area known as the 'Toxteth Triangle', which represents the heart of the drug dealing activity in the area. Granby Street dissects the 'Triangle' and is the prime site for drug dealers. "Customers" travel from outside Liverpool, some from London and Manchester, to purchase drugs. Other significant offences such as robbery, incidents involving violence and burglary take place here. The overriding factor in policing any aspect of Toxteth, in particular Granby Street, is the potential for public disorder which has dogged the area since the disturbances in 1981.

Initiatives and operations

The overall aim of the Merseyside Police Toxteth Section, made up of the Pro-Active Teams and a Community Section and responsible for policing the area, is to:

> "...take control of Granby Street, to create an environment where the community feel free from intimidation and which will encourage economic growth to return to the area."

High profile targeted patrolling - the Pro-Active Teams

In December 1993 a vigorous enforcement strategy was initiated to 'reclaim' the Granby Street area and end unlawful and anti-social behaviour. Drug dealing at the time was blatant and individuals would frequently obstruct traffic whilst conducting deals.

Four 'Pro-Active Teams' (one per shift), consisting of a mobile unit of a Sergeant and four PCs, patrol Granby Street and the immediate vicinity between the hours of eight am and two am. This approach is not to be confused with a 'swamp' type operation: the teams primarily target prioritised offences. Objectives are agreed between the teams and the Area Commander, on the basis of observations and intelligence gathered by the teams. This joint decision making is considered important by the Commander in encouraging officers to adopt a problem oriented approach. Initial targets included the cessation of street drug dealing, obstructive double parking and the driving of stolen vehicles. As dealers switched to dealing from inside premises in the Granby Street area, the identification of such premises became the next objective. Once agreed, objectives are pursued vigorously. Whilst still seeking to minimise confrontation, the fear of a public disorder incident no longer dissuades the police intervening where criminal behaviour is taking place. The duty team is able to call upon public order support units if an intervention meets significant resistance.

A 'team' will spend most of its time patrolling the quarter of a square mile that is the 'Toxteth triangle', focusing primarily on Granby Street and occasionally parking up and observing certain locations. In the first two months of operation the teams made 106 stop and searches, compared to 96 for the previous 12 months. Ninety two arrests were made with 74 offences being detected, 49 for drug possession, 12 for public disorder.

Preventive strategy - the Community Section

In addition to the more 'vigorous' target oriented policing provided by the Pro-Active Teams, Toxteth is also policed by a community foot team of sixteen officers (Inspector, Sergeant, fourteen constables).

A turning point for police-community relations was the killing in October 1992 of two young children by 'joy riders' in Granby Street. The community was galvanised into confronting the criminal and anti-social behaviour in the area. This provided an opportunity for the residents and the police to unite in a common purpose and led to the Toxteth Section developing various community initiatives.

To provide a focus for community liaison initiatives, shop premises were converted into the Granby Community Resource Centre in 1993. Based in Granby Street, the Centre functions as a police office and provides premises for numerous community groups. As well as providing a permanent police presence in the area, the sharing of premises allows officers and community activists and residents to get to know each other and exchange information. Despite its hazardous location, the Centre has only been attacked once by a 'ram raider', when damage was minimal. In October 1994 a free police and community newspaper ('Pathway') was produced by officers at the Centre, providing a forum to inform residents of police concerns and control the development of misinformed rumours. Equally, it involves residents by asking them to write articles.

Since 1990 Merseyside Police Toxteth Section, in collaboration with Merseyside Probation Service, have run a number of activity programmes for young people to be taken out of the inner city environment and participate in outdoor pursuits. An essential element of the programme is the discussion between officers and participants concerning crime and its effect on the community. The non-confrontational environment aims to ensure that whilst officers do not lecture youths, the participants are encouraged to think about issues such as drug abuse, police powers, car crime, anti-social behaviour and their effect on the community and individual life prospects. In groups of ten, two hundred and ten young people participate in the scheme every six months.

In going beyond a diversion scheme, the project is being developed to provide individuals with awards (eg. Duke of Edinburgh) and testimonials to assist employment prospects, thus providing a long term incentive to youths to participate and keep out of trouble.

Evidence of turnaround

The police view is that any attempt to reduce crime in Toxteth and the Granby Street area faces an uphill struggle. However, many crime indicators indicate the beginning of an overall improvement in Toxteth generally and the Granby Street area in particular. Recorded crime figures are shown in table 1.

Table 1: Recorded crime and % changes[1] for the Toxteth 'Triangle' and the Toxteth area				
	Toxteth 'Triangle'		Toxteth[2]	
	1993	1994	1993	1994
Burglary (dwelling)	63	61 (–3%)	332	339 (+2%)
Robbery	38	24 (–37%)	137	112 (–18%)
Theft from person	9	1 (–89%)	46	16 (–65%)
Theft from motor vehicle	10	8 (–20%)	63	79 (+25%)
Theft of motor vehicle	17	9 (–47%)	94	110 (+17%)
Incidents involving violence	53	46 (–13%)	154	141 (–8%)
Total crime figure[3]	326	267 (–18%)	1452	1490 (+3%)

Notes:

[1] NB. Caution should be exercised as some percentage changes are based on a very small number of incidents.

[2] These figures include those for 'Triangle' area. Actual figures for May 1994 were unobtainable due to a change in the recording system. Therefore an average monthly figure for 1994 was calculated and inserted for the month of May.

[3] The 'total crime' figure comprises the offence categories of: violence offences; sexual offences; burglarly (dwelling and other); robbery; theft (person); theft (bike); theft from vehicle; theft of vehicle; arson/criminal damage; 'other offences'.

In examining the impact of the initiatives on recorded crime, it can be seen that both property crime and offences against the person fell in the Granby Street area (Toxteth 'Triangle'), which may be expected as it was the focus of the police activity. However, the impact of the initiatives on the wider Toxteth area are mixed. The drop in robbery and theft from person in the wider Toxteth area does indicate that the fall in crime against the person has spread beyond the 'Triangle', although the car crime figures equally suggest a displacement effect for vehicle crime.

In addition to a reduction in recorded crime the amount of intelligence generated by the teams in intercepting vehicles and individuals was deemed invaluable by the police in developing a picture of the local and regional links of the Toxteth dealers.

After approximately five or sixth months the feeling of the teams was that policing activity was being 'allowed'. Prior to the Pro-Active Team initiative, an attempt to make an arrest would frequently have been challenged, with the possibility of violence and public disorder. As a result of the team's reputation for being polite but not backing down when faced with a crowd, arrests and other interventions are now generally only met with occasional verbal abuse.

Whilst the immediate impact of the community youth programme is difficult to measure, the police that administer the scheme believe that of over six hundred participants in the past two years, only about six have subsequently come to the attention of the police. Numerous testimonials from local resident and community groups have been received regarding the benefits of the scheme. The police recognise that street enforcement cannot alone provide an adequate or long term solution to the problems in the area and the youth and community initiatives are accorded a high priority.

Broxtowe Estate, Nottingham

This case study illustrates the application of a broad range of initiatives to a medium sized estate with problems stemming from an unusually large proportion of unemployed youths.

The Broxtowe Estate is a 1930s council estate on the edge of the city of Nottingham. It is somewhat isolated due to its poor road links with the city and has a negative reputation within the city. The 2,280 properties are mostly semi-detached, 25% being owner occupied.

The key problems on the estate are 'joy riding' (TWOC - taking of a vehicle without consent), burglary and vandalism, particularly to void (empty) properties. 'Joy riding' has become a problem for the estate partly due to the road layout which provides a ready 'racing circuit'. Another significant concern was the gathering of youths at a pedestrian entrance to the adjacent Broxtowe Country Park and damage to nearby properties. By removing bollards at this entrance 'joy riders' were able to drive onto the park after their 'displays' and dump, normally setting alight, the stolen vehicles. This entrance to the park is an established meeting place for local youths and represented a 'triangular' focus of problems for local residents and the police in terms of criminal damage, noise and public order incidents. To prevent vehicular access to the park (and the subsequent dumping of vehicles) the police and the council Parks Division secured the entrance by the positioning of very large rocks. Whilst this did prevent the dumping of vehicles on the park, the rocks became popular with the youths who used them as seating platforms, thus still encouraging this location as a focus for activity. This area became known as 'the rock(s)'.

Initiatives and operations

Prior to the mounting of the initiatives discussed below, the police met with various local agencies to co-ordinate a partnership approach. Meeting with local authority Nuisance and Harassment Officers, a joint list of problems and initiatives was drawn up. Before beginning Operation Gooseberry (discussed below) the police met with the Crown Prosecution Service and discussed issues regarding the video surveillance and evidential requirements. A joint media strategy with the local authority provided journalists with as much information as operationally possible to ensure the scope of the problem was made clear to residents and explained the need for police intervention.

High profile policing

During May and June a high profile policing strategy was adopted with more foot patrols and the deployment of traffic, dog and horse support units. Police initially focused on the heart of the estate but then moved to the outskirts of the area. This was to displace remaining offending back to the centre of the estate, the 'rocks', which was then the subject of Operation Gooseberry.

Operation Gooseberry

Operation Gooseberry was established with the intention of arresting a number of 'joy riders' and dispersing youths away from the 'rocks'. During June 1994 a covert surveillance operation was established on the 'rocks' for 22 days, between the hours of peak activity, 1pm-10pm. Following work by the Field Intelligence Officer (including ANACAPA analysis[1]) fifteen arrests were made on 1 July 1994 for

---

[1]   ANACAPA is a computerised intelligence analysis application which identifies links and relationships between various variables such as individuals, vehicles, telephone numbers etc.

offences including taking a vehicle without consent, driving a stolen motorbike, violent disorder and burglary. Fourteen youths were convicted, 13 from the Broxtowe Estate. Most pleaded guilty after seeing the quality of the video evidence against them.

Journalists were permitted to accompany the police on raids. This ensured dramatic high profile coverage of police actions. Subsequent reporting highlighted further police actions and the possibility of evictions and injunctions by the local authority for anti-social behaviour.

Police and council partnership - challenging the hotspot

Actions regarding the 'rocks' have taken on a symbolic importance as a struggle for 'control' of the area between the youths and the authorities. Despite Operation Gooseberry youths still congregated at this point. To further counter these gatherings situational design measures have been implemented. The 'rocks' themselves have been broken down to smaller boulders, which do not serve as seating platforms but still prevent vehicular access. Lighting has been improved in the area to remove the cover of darkness for illegal activity and thereby making the site less attractive as a gathering point. A speed 'barrier' was located directly at the head of the site to disrupt 'displays', though this in fact became a target of the 'joy riders' rather than a deterrent.

Various measures arising from police and council liaison have emerged as important elements in tackling the problems, with action being taken throughout the estate.

- An extensive traffic calming scheme was introduced to counter 'joy riding'.

- Abandoned vehicles are removed as soon as possible so they do not act as 'trophies' for offenders. On one occasion, within 12 hours of the police reporting a dumped vehicle the Parks Department had removed it and blocked the point of entry to the country park.

- A rapid repair policy has been adopted to counter the vandalism of street lighting, particularly at the 'rocks'.

A change in council letting policy has reduced the time between old and new tenants from an average of 7.6 to 1.2 weeks. This greatly reduces the number of void properties which are potential targets of criminal damage and arson.

Pulse-policing

One-day pulse (also known as swamp or crackdown) operations are conducted once a month in a different beat area, each focusing on a particular offence or problem. The first dealt with vehicle tax. Each operation is undertaken by the eight Permanent Beat Officers (from the other beat areas), the Community Sergeant and any available Special Constables.

A related strategy is the adoption of frequent high profile walkabouts. This is simply the local Permanent Beat Officer, sometimes accompanied by the local Inspector, undertaking a standard patrol but wearing a reflective 'traffic' jacket. The officers are clearly more visible and residents often think a 'special operation' is underway due to the special issue uniform.

Witness intimidation

Witness intimidation does exist on the estate and is met by a strong response from the authorities. To record attacks, the police have installed covert CCTV cameras and video equipment in the house of one resident following previous incidents. Lesser threats are met with the issuing of Home Office short wave panic alarms.

Another protective measure is the adoption of an alias for witness statements given to defence lawyers, the real identity being revealed only on the day of the case, thus reducing the opportunity for prior intimidation.

Evidence of turnaround

Table 2 compares recorded crime in the six months following the high profile patrolling and Operation Gooseberry with the same period in 1993. Reductions in crime can be seen for dwelling burglary, 'joy riding' (TWOC) and especially theft from vehicles (TFMV). These benefits have to be set aside an increase in arson/criminal damage and violent crime. Overall recorded crime for these offences was down 15% over the same period in the previous year.

Table 2: Recorded crime and % changes for the Broxtowe Estate (July-December 1993 and 1994)		
	1993 (2nd half)	**1994 (2nd half)**
Burglary (dwelling)	254	208 (−18%)
TWOC	63	52 (−17%)
Theft from vehicles	96	38 (−60%)
Arson/criminal damage	95	121 (+27%)
Violent crime	49	53 (+8%)
Total	557	472 (−15%)
Note: Caution should be exercised as some percentage changes are based on a very small number of incidents.		

Figures 1 and 2 show more precisely the impact of the initiatives on crime. Figure 1 details the monthly pattern of vehicle crime, one of the most significant problems on the estate, from January-December 1994.

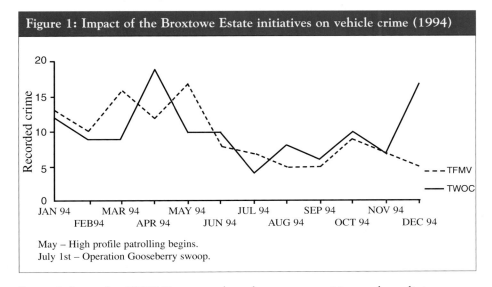

Figure 1: Impact of the Broxtowe Estate initiatives on vehicle crime (1994)

May – High profile patrolling begins.
July 1st – Operation Gooseberry swoop.

Figure 1 shows that TWOC seems to have been very sensitive to the policing operations, reducing in both months when the operations were mounted (May and July). The number of incidents remained low until the end of the year when a peak of similar size to that seen before the operations occurred. Figure 1 also shows that the reduction in theft from vehicles is associated with the police operations. Although this problem does not seem to have responded with quite the same immediacy to the operations as TWOC, the lower rate of thefts has been sustained throughout the period.

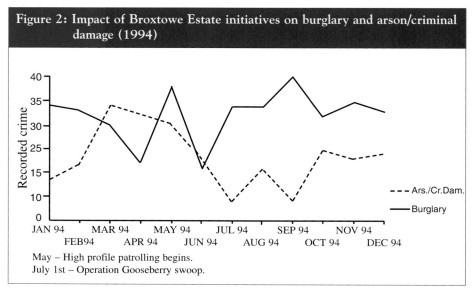

Figure 2: Impact of Broxtowe Estate initiatives on burglary and arson/criminal damage (1994)

May – High profile patrolling begins.
July 1st – Operation Gooseberry swoop.

Figure 2 shows the patterns for dwelling burglary and arson/criminal damage.

It is difficult to conclude from figure 2 that the policing operations have contributed much to the reduction in burglary which was shown in table 2. Arson/criminal damage does, however, seem to have fallen as a result of the operations, and although it did rise towards the end of the year it did not reach the levels seen prior to the initiative.

Two members of a local residents association stated to the researcher at a local multi-agency meeting that following the swoop operation, an immediate improvement was felt, the fall in 'joy riding' making for a quieter and more relaxed environment. They felt also that things were starting to be done and the feelings of isolation and abandonment amongst residents had lessened.

Kingsmead Estate, London

This case study highlights two enforcement strategies. Firstly, the targeting of key offenders and secondly, the use of civil legislation in partnership with the local authority.

The Kingsmead Estate is a 17 acre estate of 1084 dwellings in the Borough of Hackney, East London. The estate, built in 1936, is made up of 16 five-storey walk-up blocks, the eight largest occupying the central part of the estate and the remaining smaller blocks arranged along the perimeter.

The key problems on this large, isolated and self-contained estate are burglary, robbery and witness intimidation. In 1992, almost all of these problems, according to police officers, council officials and residents, stemmed from a group of approximately ten juveniles, three of whom were brothers. There was small scale drug dealing on the estate although this was not the source problem. Crime escalated in 1992, with properties being burgled in daylight in front of witnesses and threats being made against council employees. As the confidence of the offenders increased, the crime situation spiralled and residents' confidence in the police and the council plummeted. A high level of intimidation against victims and witnesses hampered any police intervention which relied on information from the public.

Initiatives and operations

In December 1992, following a number of serious assaults on residents and a council worker, a joint 'Think Tank Team' was established, comprising senior housing and police officers. This joint team set out the following objectives and strategy:-

a)   To re-investigate all burglaries and robberies committed on the estate over the previous 6 months, totalling over 250 allegations of crime. These were crimes reported by witnesses during interviews but who refused to make formal statements and the incidents were thus not officially recorded.

The 250 reports were re-investigated to gather evidence and to reassure the residents that the police and council were serious about tackling the problems on the estate.

b)   To run a parallel surveillance operation in respect of allegations of drug dealing.

'Operation Boston' began in January 1993 with 24 hour video surveillance on a target property. A month of video evidence was then supplemented by conventional surveillance. At the end of January 1993 the residents of the flat, who were known problem tenants on the estate, were arrested and charged. Three were later convicted for robbery, burglary and drug offences.

c)   To commence proceedings for the eviction of, and serving of exclusion orders against, tenants abusing their tenancy through criminality.

Running in parallel to the police operation, the housing enforcement team prepared a civil course of action. Following the criminal convictions police evidence was made available to enable the local authority to take civil action. Injunctions, forbidding the entering of the estate, were served in May 1993 against five defendants, four of them from one family associated with the target flat in Operation Boston.

Hackney Housing Department Tenancy Audit Team

Established in the autumn of 1991, the Tenancy Audit Team (TAT) is a local authority housing department investigation and enforcement unit. The TAT became involved with the Kingsmead project and were able to offer detailed information about the estate's residents to the police. During their investigations, which ran parallel to the local CID, they were often able to obtain information not given to the detective team because of their non-police status and broader concerns regarding the estate and its residents.

The TAT operates out of a discreet council property, which helps overcome the fear of witness and victim intimidation, encouraging individuals to attend and give statements (to the TAT and the police) if they do not wish to be visited at home or visit a police station. "The general feeling on the estate is that the police are not discreet and people reporting crimes become known to the gang who retaliate later" (victim statement to the TAT, December 1992). Following the serving of the injunctions in May 1993, the TAT also monitored the estate for evidence of the orders being breached.

The TAT have developed an in-house computer system to detect frauds and multiple accommodation applications or tenancies. The system allows the identification of potential problem 'hot spots' eg. if 40% of a council residential block is void this may indicate (or give rise to) problems in the block. The TAT are also able to locate individuals, a facility they extend to the police. This co-operation helps the authorities deal with serious problem and criminal tenants and engenders a positive relationship between the police and the local authority.

Information on the location or actions of problem individuals is also received from other residents. The majority of resident information is received via unsolicited phone calls though TAT officers maintain close contacts with individuals on the estate. Occasionally a TAT officer may introduce a resident to a local CID officer who may develop an independent relationship with the tenant.

Civil legislation

The use of injunctions provides interim relief and can be an important weapon against witness and victim intimidation, a major factor in the problems on the Kingsmead estate. Injunctions were undertaken under Section 222 of the Local Government Act 1972 which provides local authorities with the power to prosecute:

> '(1) Where a local authority consider(s) it expedient for the promotion or protection of the interests of the inhabitants of their area-'

Once served in May 1993 the injunctions prohibited named individuals:

a) entering of properties on the estate;

b) causing damage to council property; and

c) assaulting or threatening council employees or estate residents.

Affidavits can be used in applying for injunctions, though if challenged (and here they were, funded by legal aid) then witness cross examination may be required. To try and minimise potential intimidation, witnesses who had since moved off the estate were able to keep their address confidential (with the permission of the Judge).

Police co-operation

In conducting these and subsequent operations, a close relationship developed between the TAT and the police. Police evidence and statements were passed to the TAT, after the criminal prosecution, to assist the obtaining of injunctions and evictions. Once the injunctions were served the local beat officer played an important role in enforcing the injunction by reporting any breach of the order (eg. if an individual under notice was seen on the estate).

Estate Policing

In dealing with problems on the estate the local Permanent Beat Officer (PBO) meets with the estate housing manager who maintains a register of resident reported anti-social and nuisance behaviour. Incidents or potentially problem tenants can then be discussed and co-ordinated remedial action taken. The PBO also participates in various community projects such as the youth football scheme.

Crime on Estates Working Group

Following the police and council operations concerning the Kingsmead estate in 1993 a joint Crime on Estates Working Group was established by Hackney council in January 1995 to identify problem areas throughout the borough and co-ordinate multi-agency action. Issues discussed include:

•   Pirate radio stations in the borough.

•   Prostitution.

•   Summer diversion schemes.

•   Crime and nuisance monitoring on estates.

Community oriented programmes

Attempting to build on the beginnings of improved relations following police and council efforts to tackle the problems of the estate, long term objectives were based around the establishment of the Kingsmead Community Trust in June 1993, part of a wide-ranging community regeneration programme. A permanent police input into this aspect of community improvement is provided by their presence on the Management Board of the Community Trust. This participation enables the police to remain informed of community initiatives, problems and tensions. Equally an opportunity is provided for the police to put across their concerns and explain their actions.

Evidence of turnaround

Table 3: Recorded crime and % changes for the Kingsmead Estate (1992-1994)			
	1992	1993	1994
Burglary	139	43 (–69%)	85 (+98%)
Robbery	24	19 (–21%)	15 (–21%)
Arson	9	3 (–66%)	4 (+33%)
Vehicle crime (theft of & from)	45	31 (–31%)	45 (+45%)
Violence against the person	7	17 (+142%)	25 (+47%)

Note:
Caution should be exercised as some percentage changes are based on a very small number of incidents.

The reduction in burglary following the arrests from Operation Boston in January 1993 is clearly shown in table 3. The total number of domestic burglaries fell dramatically in 1993 but rose in 1994, though still 39% down on 1992 (pre-operation period). A comparison of the six months prior to the Operation (August 1992 - January 1993) and the six months following (February 1993 - July 1993) indicate a fall from an average of fourteen burglaries a month to three a month. The reason put forward by local police and the TAT for the rise in burglaries was that another large criminal family living on the estate had become active in the area now that the previous family and gang had been removed.

Incidents of robbery fell throughout 1993 and 1994 to a 37.5% decrease on 1992, although the numbers are small. Comparison between the six months prior to the operation with the six months afterwards shows a fall from an average of three robberies a month to just over one a month.

In contrast to these reductions offences of violence against the person showed a two and a half times increase in 1993 (though based on only seven incidents in 1992) and a further increase in 1994. The reason for this is unclear though it may be that with a reduced fear of intimidation, residents were more prepared to report assaults against them. Vehicle crime (including theft of and theft from) fell in 1993, though rose again in 1994 to 1992 levels.

Another indicator, albeit anecdotal, of improvement is that the TAT reported that residents were actively offering their flats as observation sites to the TAT - in 1992 residents were reluctant to even talk to them.

Voids

On the Kingsmead Estate voids were sometimes used for storing stolen property or were broken into and vandalised, occasionally being set alight. To counter these problems void properties were protected by metal door and window screens. Because of the poor reputation of the Kingsmead and the negative impression given by such screens, potential tenants were put off living on the estate, which in turn reinforced the cycle of empty properties.

Following the high profile crime crack-down in January 1993 and the actions of the TAT in identifying squatters, coupled with an intense estate management approach, the number of voids has dropped significantly - from 262 in April 1993 to 63 in May 1995, a drop of 76%. The block where the key offenders lived and, along with the block opposite, where they offended most, had void levels of 45%. With the removal of the problem family (who occupied one flat), the void level in the two blocks has dropped to 12%. The estate manager is convinced that the fall in voids is due to a large extent to the uptake of properties by new tenants aware that the concerted council and police action has brought about a change for the better on the estate.

Gateshead, Newcastle

Another example of co-operation between local police and specialist housing officers exists between the Tenancy Enforcement Team (TET) of Gateshead Metropolitan Borough Council Housing Department and Gateshead Area East police.

In early 1994 the Housing Committee of Gateshead Metropolitan Borough Council decided to establish the Tenancy Enforcement Team to tackle growing criminal and anti-social behaviour on council housing estates. It was noted that whilst the final sanction of eviction was possible under the nuisance clause of council residents' Tenancy Agreements it was time consuming and more importantly, very few actions had been able to proceed "because of the real fears of reprisal felt [by resident witnesses and victims] despite assistance and encouragement from [housing] officers." Centralising Housing Department actions regarding problem tenants through the provision of a dedicated team also distanced local housing staff from enforcement actions. Housing officers were often located on the estate, and were increasingly subject to threatening behaviour whilst dealing with complaints.

The Tenancy Enforcement Team

The TET has a comprehensive remit to:

a) contact victims of criminal and/or anti-social behaviour on council estates;

b) liaise with relevant agencies and council departments;

c) develop swift and effective problem resolving strategies;

d) gather suitable evidence, including witness statements;

e) assist in the preparation of Legal Notices where appropriate; and

f) attend court hearings.

Training for TET officers included mediation skills with the North East Mediation Service and static surveillance techniques from the police.

In interviewing victims and witnesses the TET will meet individuals "any place, any time" and attend homes disguised as workmen. Such flexibility is essential to overcome fears of, and prevent, intimidation by offenders. Observation is also undertaken using camcorders and time lapse recording systems.

An anonymous phone-line for complaints and information regarding anti-social or criminal behaviour by tenants is operated via an answering machine. The number of the phone-line is given only to potential victim tenants in 'high risk areas'. In the first four months of use 31 anonymous calls were received.

Problem Tenant Registry

The TET maintain a central registry of anti-social incidents and individuals on a card index system. Problem areas or tenants can be monitored and identified quickly to allow either early intervention or support later legal action if required.

Police co-operation with the TET

Police co-operation consists of:

a) Identifying problem residents.

b)   Supplying information to support civil actions.

c)   Warning problem tenants of potential council action.

The Housing Department and the local Superintendent together identified the ten most problematic families on the estate so as to "concentrate on the most criminal and anti-social households rather than diffusing the effort". Day to day TET liaison with the police is via the sector Inspector or a contact officer in the Intelligence Unit, although meetings may involve the Superintendent Divisional Commander if required.

Assisting civil actions: disclosure and follow up

Having assisted in identifying a target list of ten families the police then disclosed information which would support any council civil action such as an injunction or, in the last resort, an eviction application. Currently, disclosed information relating to individuals includes incident calls, arrests, charges and convictions.

The exchange of information has recently been enhanced by the flagging of target individuals. Any logged incident which involves an individual or address on the problem resident list is automatically brought to the attention of the sector Inspector. A vetting process occurs at this stage and only information considered non-sensitive and relevant to the TET remit is passed on.

Operationally, joint pressure can be brought to bear on problem tenants by following up police attendance at an incident with the following:

a)   Police inform TET of attendance (subject to vetting).

b)   Inspector tells the tenant that the Housing Department have been informed and that he/she may be in breach of their Tenancy Agreement.

c)   The TET inform the tenant that an incident has been brought to their attention and the incident may be investigated.

An aspect of such action, stressed by both the police and the TET, is that incidents and complaints are followed up rapidly. Thus a tenant would receive two formal warning letters (one from the police and one from the council) within a week of a criminal or anti-social incident occurring. The exchange of information is carried out on a daily basis, shaped by operational requirements rather than timetabled monthly meetings.

Operational performance

Up to May 1995 no evictions had occurred. Of the original ten target families or individuals, seven left the estate voluntarily, two ceased their anti-social behaviour and one individual was taken into care. Since its formation, in June 1994, and February 1995 the TET has received notification of 413 individuals, with the following actions:

Table 4: Operational results of the TET (June 1994-February 1995)	
ACTION TAKEN	**No.**
Interviews and statements taken	186
Notices of intent to repossess served	40
Legal warning letter issued	7
Formal interview with senior housing officers	6
RESULTS OF SUCH ACTIONS	**No.**
Offender(s) (non-tenants) left home	27
Flits and terminations	40
Possession proceedings initiated by the council	10
No re-offending	41
Evictions	nil

Note:
The number of 'Actions taken' is greater than the 'Results' because interviews and statements includes both complainants, 'defendants' and witnesses.

As a result of information provided to the police by the TET during the period 1 June - 1 October 1994, 12 arrests were made, 8 charges brought with 6 convictions or cautions. Of the 41 individuals or families recorded as having not re-offended as of March 1995, the TET estimate that only 5-6 had subsequently come to their notice again by January 1996.

Meadow Well Estate, Newcastle

This case study serves as an example of a 'community policing' strategy, explicitly developed around the concept of 'problem oriented policing' (Goldstein, 1991).

The Meadow Well Estate is north east of Newcastle. Built alongside the industrial village of Percy Main, the properties are primarily 1970s semi-detached houses with gardens. As of January 1994 the estate comes under the large A19 Area of the Northumbria Police, though previously and for the time of this study, the estate was policed by a dedicated Community Policing Unit.

The Meadow Well Estate achieved prominence following a night of serious public disorder in September 1991 which led to the destruction of local shops, a youth centre and violent clashes with police. The riots were sparked by misinformation regarding police involvement in the accidental death of two 'joy riders'.

The key crimes on the estate were burglary, 'joy riding', vandalism and general juvenile nuisance. Intimidation was a significant problem. The greatest concern regarding the estate however was the deterioration of relations between the police and the community, not just the youth.

Community Policing Unit

Following the disturbances of September 1991 and the immediate 'swamp' police presence which followed, a dedicated Unit was assigned to the estate. Becoming operational in November 1991 the Unit consisted of a sergeant (Unit head) and 12 constables operating initially out of a room in the neighbourhood Health Clinic. In April 1992, with additional funding from the 1992-1993 Urban Crime Fund Initiative, the Unit was increased by an inspector, two detective constables (who were withdrawn in November 1993) and four civilian staff. The Unit for the Meadow Well Estate was relocated to permanent accommodation in a building shared with the local Housing and Social Services Departments. Officers operated over two shifts covering 8am to midnight.

In the aftermath of the disturbances and the stand-off between the community and the police, it was recognised that the policing strategy for the area had to be reviewed and the local commander decided to adopt a long term 'problem oriented' approach. The philosophy of the Unit was based on six key concepts, detailed in table 5 below.

Table 5: Philosophy of the Community Policing Unit
1   **A quality personalised service.** Become involved in the community, get to know the customers and let them get to know you. Become a village Bobby.
2   **Customer orientation.** Identify the customers' priorities and align the organisation's priorities to theirs. Don't impose services because the organisation knows best.
3   **Problem solving.** Idenfity, analyse, respond, evaluate. Try to get to the root cause of the problem rather than the quick fix. Think laterally, be innovative, don't be bound by previous approaches.
4   **Devolution of authority to the shop floor.** Empower staff by removing the fear of making mistakes and encourage discretion.
5   **Ownership.** Officers must feel that they can make a difference and put themselves into the job, ie utilise all their skills and abilities not just those that complement law enforcement.
6   **Proactive rather than reactive.** Identify emerging problems and deploy resources to tackle the source.

The team spent a day discussing and drawing up the objectives of the Unit, which were to:

a) Identify the problems in the area by proactive, frequent, non-confrontational contact and communication with residents of all ages.

b) Reduce crime, by identifying/targeting offenders and offences, and the vigorous investigation of offences.

c) Provide intensive and directed uniformed patrols in the area.

d) Improve the quality of life for residents by reducing the fear of crime and disorder, enhancing public confidence in the police and developing improved police/public relations.

In practice these strategic objectives and underlying philosophy were translated into nine operational tactics:

1) Be open and honest with the public, fully explaining actions when necessary.

By attending, with the council, fortnightly resident 'street meetings' and numerous tenants associations, the officers took every opportunity to meet and talk with residents. This allowed officers to develop a knowledge of individuals' and tenants' concerns and to engage in rumour control by tackling false allegations and explaining police actions.

2) Give officers responsibility for their own time management.

3) Allow officers wider discretion.

Applying the problem oriented approach of the Unit, officers were given the discretion to implement strategies in their allocated area as they saw fit. Their time was their own and they were encouraged to take a broader and more creative approach to meeting the overall objectives. Supervisors became advisors, giving guidance rather than instruction. An officer commented, "I think the discretion is tremendous, given the responsibility you then realise it's your personal problem, and you've got to take ownership of the estate. Not until you do that do you feel a part of it and that's where the job satisfaction comes in" (Goddard and Walker, 1993). To encourage this attitude management had to convince officers that mistakes stemming from experimental initiatives would be genuinely tolerated and seen as part of a learning process for the whole Unit.

4) Visit schools and youth clubs.

Cited as one of the most important functions for the Unit, each local school and youth club was assigned to a specific officer who patrolled that area. A resident commented, "They have got to get into the schools and the community, kids have got to know police you can trust: police who are human, not just there to lock you up." (Goddard and Walker, 1993). Officers organised school trips, football coaching and other activities such as Outward Bound courses. Such activities invoked ownership of youth problems in that they draw upon personal skills not law enforcement ability, eg an officer showing himself as a canoe instructor rather than a policeman.

5) Get involved in community activities.

6) Help the development of community spirit.

Officers took part in every community forum and activity available to try and establish better relations with residents. A resident commented, "The voluntary police [the Unit] spoke to us, asked us to give them a chance, everybody gave them a chance, and we got a good response. The kids speak to them. They've gone out of their way, they've done more than they had to." (Goddard and Walker, 1993). This involved supporting activities such as bingo and day trips for pensioners on the estate. For the young, inter-school sports competitions were held. The Unit sergeant also wrote a column in the community newspaper. Fun days were held and children posed (and paid) for pictures with mounted and motorcycle police officers.

The Unit used only unmarked vehicles to patrol the estate, so as to enable their additional use as community transport - as one officer put it "Doing things for people rather than Doing (sic) people for things". The provision of such transport was seen as a major form of non-confrontational contact. Although not its intention, the use of unmarked vehicles caused residents to distinguish 'their' police from 'North Shields' (divisional headquarters). For a community that had always felt abandoned by the authorities to receive a dedicated police team, despite the poor relations with the service, was an indicator that at last attention was being paid to them.

7) Work with other statutory agencies.

The Unit originally shared accommodation with the local Housing office and Social Services. Familiarity between the staff and officers came about through informal contact as well as facilitating formal liaison when required. It also provided a cover for anyone wishing to contact the police, otherwise problematic because of the fear of witness intimidation. People would sometimes report incidents to the Housing manager who would then persuade them to talk to an officer (normally in her presence) who could simply walk downstairs. The Housing Office has now been relocated and the Housing Manager considers a significant opportunity for improved communication has been lost.

8) Encourage a cleaner environment.

'Litter picks' with the young children were carried out in certain areas of the estate.

9) The attitude of all Meadow Well officers is to be based on a policy of being 'fair, firm and friendly'.

Although the Unit spent much of its time getting to know the community via social activities, a high profile police enforcement presence was a strategic objective. To progress community relations however, certain activity was tolerated such as the riding of untaxed and uninsured motorcycles on the estate, on the way to local waste ground.

Underpinning all objectives and tactics was the re-establishment of trust in police-resident relations:

> "The Unit police officers described the climate in the early stages of the initiative as one where there was no trust for the police and open hostility was common - adults were said to totally ignore officers or pass derogatory comments, 'whilst the kids might snort at you, or occasionally throw a stone or two'. Faced with this situation the Unit decided that the only way forward was to go out on foot, speak to people and try to establish trust. They attempted to go to every and any public forum and went to meeting after meeting in order to spread their philosophy." (Goddard and Walker, 1993)

Another aspect of frequent and frank contact with residents, was that officers themselves learnt to overcome their views about residents. An officer commented, "I came in with strong opinions of what type of people live on this estate. I've softened though. Because I have time to spend with them, I've gained an understanding of their problems." (Goddard and Walker, 1993).

Problem solving

Two examples illustrate how proactive measures can be developed and the personal knowledge of officers drawn upon in attempting a problem solving approach.

Witness intimidation and tenant harassment are major problems on the estate, a difficulty exacerbated by the low number of private and public telephones. The Safelink Experiment commenced in May 1992 to "encourage and reassure witnesses and persons suffering extreme harassment" by the provision (courtesy of Vodaphone) of a modified mobile phone. In assessing their effectiveness the Unit concluded the initiative had been good in reassuring witnesses though the phones had not actually encouraged more individuals to come forward. The initiative is however being replicated in other problem areas of Newcastle.

On another occasion an elderly couple were greatly distressed, believing that someone was trying to burgle their home after their burglar alarm was repeatedly activated. The officers who attended the home believed that an electrical fault was the cause of the alarm activations and asked another officer with experience in electrical work to check the system, where a fault was found.

Policing - Partnership with the Community

To promote good police-community relations the local Superintendent held two half day consultation seminars during 1994, where the police, agency officials and resident representatives discussed community issues. Possible action plans discussed the maintenance of visible foot patrols, schools liaison and the expectation that possible solutions must be seen as long term.

Evidence of turnaround

Before discussing evidence of an improvement in the estate it must be noted that changes other than the establishment of the Community Policing Unit were taking place during the time of this case study. Certain key offenders were imprisoned following the disturbances and areas of the estate became depopulated as houses were demolished and new resident developments built.

Recorded crime

Table 6: Recorded crime and % change for the Meadow Well Estate 1991-1994				
	1991	1992	1993	1994
Burglary	423	193 (–54%)	146 (–24%)	221 (+51%)
Criminal damage	224	156 (–54%)	205 (+32%)	164 (–20%)
Theft from vehicles	134	61 (–54%)	65 (+7%)	133 (+104%)
Theft of vehicles	89	47 (–47%)	86 (+84%)	77 (–10%)
Stolen vehicles abandoned on the estate*	225	184 (–18%)	158 (–14%)	104 (–34%)

Note:
Caution should be exercised as some percentage changes are based on a very small number of incidents.

*This is not a recorded crime category, but was recorded by the CPU as part of a monitoring exercise.

The reduction in burglary of dwellings following the September 1991 disturbances is clearly illustrated in table 6. The number of recorded burglaries fell in 1992 and 1993 and rose in 1994, though still representing a 48% reduction on 1991. One explanation for this rise put forward by local officers was that a large number of burglaries occurred as a result of the theft of newly installed boilers from remodernised and newly built unoccupied homes on the estate. This problem was endemic until the council increased security measures on the building sites. A second reason for the increase in dwelling burglary may be the increasing occupation of new properties.

Criminal damage fell in 1992, rose in 1993, followed by another drop in 1994 representing an overall decrease of 27% on 1991 levels. Like burglary, much criminal damage has been aimed at the building sites and the equipment stored overnight.

A major reduction in all facets of recorded vehicle crime was seen during the Unit's first year of operation. In 1992 theft of and from vehicles fell by a half, with a major reduction in stolen vehicles recovered from the estate (an indicator of 'joy riding' activity) which continued during 1993 and 1994, representing an overall reduction of 54% on the 1991 level of abandoned vehicles. However, whilst theft from vehicles remained halved in 1993, by 1994 they had risen to 1991 levels. Theft of vehicles doubled in 1993 to the 1991 level, though fell again in 1994 with an overall reduction of 13% on 1991 levels. Two explanations are put forward for the increase in theft of and theft from vehicles in 1993 and 1994 respectively. Firstly, as a result of the extensive construction work on the estate numerous vehicles belonging to the workers were parked on and around the construction areas. Secondly, in 1994 a leisure water-park opened up near the estate (covered by the Unit) with an unprotected car park. Both these developments represent a new source of targets for local offenders.

Housing Department

Rent arrears for 1994 were down 14.9% on 1993. This is seen by the local Housing manager as indicative of the genuine improvement of relations between residents and the 'authorities' (council and police). It is seen as an indicator that residents are increasingly choosing to stay on the estate. With a stake in the future of the area, they are prepared to pay their rent and increasingly speak out in tackling criminal and nuisance behaviour.

Quality of service

A quality of service survey was undertaken by Northumbria police in 1992 to evaluate public perceptions of policing in certain areas, including the Meadow Well estate. Of the 170 residents surveyed, 13% felt more safe than they had a year previously and 77% were satisfied with the policing they had received. An independent assessment of the various initiatives in Northumbria funded by the Urban Crime Fund (UCF) reported that:

"Attitudes toward the police are more positive, and they perceive them as being prepared to consider their [residents] needs and willing to work with them in reducing crime. These changes are particularly impressive albeit that the period started with extremely negative views of policing in the area." (Goddard and Walker, 1993).

Residents interviewed by an independent assessment team (Goddard and Walker, 1993) attributed reductions in crime to three aspects of the policing strategy:

a)   The Unit's high profile deterred offenders.

b)   The police had a greater local knowledge of offenders and could target their activity accordingly.

c)   Offenders were aware that victims and witnesses were more likely to report incidents.

The crime reduction on the Meadow Well was not brought about by a dramatic surge in arrests or newly discovered 'solutions' to the problems of the area. The evidence presented here suggests that the improvements on the Meadow Well have been brought about by the Unit's increased presence, shortened response times and informed targeting of offenders. Overall, officers firmly believed that the Meadow Well was now a 'very quiet' area, producing less crime and incidents than its neighbouring estates, to which they were turning their attention. The long term future for the Unit's achievements and its subsequent incorporation into a wider command area cannot be foreseen. In 1993 the Unit's sergeant stated:

"If you were putting a house up, you could say that deep and solid foundations have been laid, no further than that, there's no structure. The timbers are being prepared by the involvement in schools, but it will take several years before they are strong enough for lasting structures....you need the time and the resources to carry on the building process. Trust got built by individuals...The force tends to make short term commitments and is in danger if the public perceive they are let down again." (Goddard and Walker, 1993).

Killingbeck, Leeds

Community Beat Managers

Another approach to facilitating a problem-oriented style of policing lies in the organisation and management of permanent or community beat officers. Although it was not possible to evaluate the impact on crime of the changes made by this division, because they had only been introduced recently and along with other policing changes, this study does illustrate the kind of changes needed to encourage beat officers to take a more strategic approach to the way they police their areas.

Beat Managers

Killingbeck Division, Leeds, has been attempting a shift towards a more proactive policing style since mid-1993. Attempts at bringing about the required cultural change from a reactive short term perspective amongst officers to long term problem oriented approach have been accompanied by organisational changes to the policing of the division.

The foundation of such change lies in the designation of the 17 Permanent Beat Officers (PBOs) as Beat Managers. The aim is to formalise and make explicit the responsibility of each officer to 'manage' his/her beat area. The PBOs are removed from the General Policing Group (standard shift cover) and thus effectively ring-fenced from being drawn upon to perform other duties to the detriment of their community initiatives. Each constable 'manager' is asked to consider:

a)   How is the area now?

b)   How would I like it to be (vision)?

c)   What objectives do I have for the coming year?

d)   What support will I need (action plan)?

Each Beat Manager is required to draw up a Beat Business Plan which forms the blueprint for the beat operational targets for the coming year. This states the officer's vision, year's objectives and action plans for the area. This annual strategy is supplemented by more specific monthly objectives and action plans. An example of a Beat Business Plan is given in appendix A.

To encourage the active implementation of such an approach by the officers the plan forms the basis of a 'contract' with the Community Liaison Inspector and is a component of the officer's annual appraisal.

As well as containing operational goals the Beat Manager is required to draw up a detailed Community Beat Profile of the area, which may include:

• crime hot spots	• community bodies/premises
• known local offenders	• 'Watch' schemes
• commercial targets	• schools, churches etc.
• licensed premises	• local officials, eg housing

The production of such a profile requires the officer to carry out the necessary research and thereby familiarise him/herself with the area. Similarly, the profile serves as an effective briefing document for a new officer taking over the beat.

Crime Prevention Strategist

To assist and enhance the adoption of such a broad responsibility by the Beat Managers, the Community Unit is supported by a dedicated Crime Prevention Strategist. The strategist represents a substantial resource for the officers to draw upon, providing crime analysis and prevention advice, when identifying objectives and action plans in their area. To encourage officers to use the strategist, he/she is located in the same work area as the Beat Managers to ensure constant and easy access.

3. Good practice

The varying initiatives described in the case studies are discussed below in three broad categories: police enforcement, civil action and community oriented measures. Such categories are broad and overlap, but are useful in providing a basic framework by which to discuss the numerous tactics identified. The discussion of 'strategy' which follows emphasises the interlocking and mutually supportive nature of short and long term actions in these three areas.

Police enforcement

Despite the variety of problems faced by, and resources available to, area commanders, certain themes emerge from the case studies as being useful to consider when making tactical choices.

Targeting offenders

The pro-active intelligence led targeting of key offenders is as viable for estate crime as for more serious offences. Although often minor, the habitual high incident and attendance levels on high crime estates take up a large amount of police resource. This approach, obtaining intelligence via surveillance or informants, may be facilitated by the fact that the areas for surveillance and the offenders are predominantly local and known to the police.

Surveillance targets may be readily apparent when offenders, often youths, frequently gather at the same locations. Intelligence should be collated and analysed with the rigour given to higher grade targets; ANACAPA analysis and Field Intelligence Officers (FIOs) were drawn upon on the Broxtowe Estate. Intelligence gathering should be seen as part of everyday policing and not left to FIOs or special operations. The Toxteth Teams view the production of intelligence logs as a routine function and have built up a detailed picture of offending and offenders in their area. The same may be done in any high crime area.

High profile targeted patrols

The adoption, where required, of a vigorous street enforcement policy can not only exist alongside community bridge building, but may facilitate such a goal. The deployment of a high profile police unit with an active enforcement remit cannot, and should not, replace the long term development of community relations. However, such an approach, as illustrated by the Toxteth Pro-Active Teams, may exist alongside, and indeed, reinforce community strategies.

Some areas face serious crime problems, such as drug dealing or prostitution, which may generate wider offending patterns. Such problems may be beyond the scope of community policing initiatives. Community groups and lone constables may be unable to tackle large scale and potentially dangerous criminal problems. The entrenched and defended drug dealing in Toxteth required a vigorous enforcement solution in the form of the Toxteth Pro-Active Teams.

In areas where communities feel abandoned, a feeling often reported, a significant display of commitment to tackling crime may be required, before residents feel confident enough to assist the police and other agencies. If the public perceive an inability or unwillingness by the authorities to act then requests for assistance by the police in community forums and actions may be undermined. High profile intervention is normally resource intensive but can be used to show a commitment from the service to the community which may then encourage wider community support. Major enforcement operations can serve as a backdrop to launch other community based initiatives.

An important caveat to such operations is that they must be seen to be legitimate by residents. Operation Gooseberry on the Broxtowe Estate involved considerable media liaison and rumour control in an effort to generate the support of the community for the policing initiatives.

Pulse policing

Crackdowns can be facilitated by the adoption of pulse policing. Problems may exist which require more than a local beat officer but the resources are not available or required for a sustained enforcement operation. Pulse policing is the deployment of a greater number of officers than is usual in an area for a short period. The impact of sustained initiatives may wear off as offenders adjust their behaviour or reevaluate the probability of detection (Sherman, 1990). When crackdowns are applied for short, irregular periods rather than regular longer intervals a deterrent effect is achieved which lasts longer than the actual operation because offenders are unable to predict when and for how long a crackdown will occur. By constantly changing the area (or offence being targeted) coverage can be maximised throughout a command area. As on the Broxtowe Estate such initiatives can be undertaken with existing resources by the temporary reassignment of beat officers and the use of Special constables.

Increased visibility

Practices to maximise public perception of a police presence may be considered a priority in light of the national objective regarding high visibility policing. Simple techniques encountered to generate a perceived increased police presence, during pulse initiatives or otherwise, included the wearing of high visibility 'traffic' jackets by foot patrols. As well as an increased visible presence literally, residents and potential offenders assumed a special operation was taking place because of the exceptional uniform.

Another Inspector set a monthly target for hours spent on foot patrol for himself and his officers. This was more effective than general exhortations to 'get out there and meet people on the pavement'. The same officer also requested that if mobile officers returning to the stations were double crewed, one of them would walk back through the estate. The Inspector would often walk back from community meetings to show a presence.

Witness intimidation

Countering witness intimidation should be a priority. Basic measures can be incorporated into general police practice with minimal resource implications. Without the support of victims and witnesses the criminal justice process falls at the first hurdle. On housing estates offenders and victims or witnesses often live close to each other. Thus the fear of, and potential for, intimidation is greatly increased. Counter-measures for witness intimidation have been suggested in previous Home Office research (Maynard, 1994). Briefly, they need to be implemented in three broad areas:

i) Reaching victims and witnesses

Witnesses must be shown that protective measures are in place to protect them if they come forward and that complaints (criminal and civil) will be followed through by all the agencies involved.

ii) Obtaining statements

Greater discretion in obtaining statements should be shown by the service. Measures suggested by Maynard (1994) include:

- A discrete radio transmission policy to prevent witness details being revealed to those who may be listening with scanners.

- Witnesses given the option of reporting to a police station or other agency premises to give a statement.

- Witnesses being visited preferably by non-uniform officers, and if possible, as one of a number of seemingly routine house to house enquiries.

The use of third parties as a go between for victims and the police should be recognised and encouraged. Residents were often found to be more willing to pass information to other agency staff such as housing officers. With the encouragement of such staff residents would provide statements to police officers, often at premises other than the local station.

iii) Providing protective measures

Various measures can be used to minimise witness intimidation once statements have been given and a case proceeds to court.

- The use of an alias and the withholding of the witness's address on statements given to the defence (with the Judge's permission).

- The use of injunctions to forbid contact or proximity between the accused and the witness (see Civil actions).

- The issuing of Home Office panic alarms or dedicated mobile phones to high risk witnesses, together with a rapid police response policy. This can be used to respond to attacks and/or to ensure the recording of an injunction breach (see Civil actions).

- Where a high or proven risk witness exists it may be necessary to provide surveillance (staffed or electronic) of the potential victim. Such evidence of intimidation can be used to support prosecution which can serve to deter further witness intimidation.

Civil actions

The police service should be aware of the potential role for the use of civil law by their local authority partners and the supportive role the police can play. By undertaking civil enforcement, a second front is being opened up to support the police regulation of problem areas. This front can run in parallel to police criminal actions.

Sanctions and mechanisms

Although evictions and injunctions are products of the civil legal process and local authority administration, the sanctions they provide can be highly effective. The threat of eviction may be a significant deterrent when publicised, and if necessary, exercised.

Injunctions may be another instrument against a variety of problem and criminal behaviours. Because of their flexibility and, in certain circumstances, speed of implementation, they are being used more by local authority legal departments.

Various statutory instruments available to local authorities for tackling problem behaviours are contained in appendix B.

Eviction

Traditionally local authorities have relied upon general 'nuisance' clauses of tenancy agreements to deal with anti-social or criminal tenants. The past ten years have seen the strengthening of such agreements by the inclusion of more detailed clauses in agreements to address harassment, nuisance and crime.

The ultimate enforcement option stemming from tenancy breaches is eviction. Eviction is viewed as a last resort by agencies because of the implications for those concerned and it is a slow and expensive procedure. Authorities therefore have increasingly been exploring the use of injunctions to restrain problem behaviour.

<u>Injunctions</u>

An injunction is a court order which can be used to require an individual, group of individuals or organisation to refrain from specified actions. This may include forbidding the breaking of specified tenancy clauses (discussed above), damaging council property, trespassing on council property (exclusion order) and assaulting council staff or specified individuals. Rather than making a formal judgement a Judge may often ask the parties to agree to an 'undertaking' by the defendant that he or she will refrain from a specified action.[2]

Various circumstances may make the use of an injunction an attractive option. These may include:

- **Provide civil enforcement where the criminal process is not possible or viable.** The evidential requirements under criminal process are such that the viability of prosecution may limit effective police intervention against problem or criminal tenants. Civil injunction actions do not need to prove intent and require a lower burden of proof ('the balance of probability' rather than 'beyond reasonable doubt'). Where a criminal action may have failed a local authority may attempt civil proceedings and utilise statements and information gathered previously by the police.

- **Represent a powerful sanction.** The sanction of potential exclusion from one's immediate social group via an exclusion order may serve as a stronger deterrent and penalty compared to a fine or suspended sentence in the criminal court.

- **Counter witness intimidation.** An injunction may forbid contact or proximity between the defendant and the witness. In the absence of the defendant being held on remand during a criminal case, or to prevent interference during a civil case, a civil injunction may be an important instrument to deter intimidation.

---

[2]   For practical purposes an undertaking is viewed as an injunction in the following discussion.

The police role in civil action

The Kingsmead Estate and Gateshead case studies provide two examples of how civil housing enforcement departments may be supported by the police. Predominantly this may be the provision of information already in the public domain and by enforcement of civil actions.

Sharing information

To help an authority prepare a case for an injunction or eviction the police might provide information regarding:

- convictions;

- arrests;

- charges;

- current proceedings;

- incident calls (involving the individual or address); and

- witness and officer statements.

Only basic details of incidents (defendant, charges) can be given where a case is sub judicie and incident logs should be screened such that only relevant and non-sensitive information is passed to the authority. When full hearings are undertaken for final eviction proceedings and defended injunctions, officers may be required to attend court and give oral evidence as in the criminal court.

Data protection

Section 28 (Crime and Taxation) of the Data Protection Act provides exemptions for the provision of information for the following purposes:

a) the prevention or detection of crime;

b) the apprehension or prosecution of offenders; or

c) the assessment or collection of any tax or duty.

Officers should always consult the force appointee responsible for Data Protection issues before entering into data exchange agreements.

Having discussed what the police can provide to civil teams it should be noted that such a partnership can involve a two way flow of information. Local authority teams may be able to provide useful knowledge to the police regarding local offenders who are also known as problem tenants.

Enforcement support

The recording and reporting of an injunction (or undertaking) breach is essential. Although a police officer can rarely arrest an individual who is violating an injunction, the incident should be reported to the local authority. Breaching an injunction represents a contempt of court and an officer's statement and pocket book entry can serve as evidence in any subsequent hearing. The use of alarms and a priority response policy can facilitate the reporting of such breaches.

Co-operating in the establishment of specialist housing enforcement teams. Agreement needs to be reached on what and how information is to be exchanged. Advice on static surveillance could also be given.

The joint identification of problems. Through monitoring similar problems by different mechanisms, the council and police may identify new issues and troublesome areas, as well as new ways of tackling them. When drawing up a joint problem priority list, both parties may receive new information regarding offending and offenders.

Facilitating operational liaison. The appointment of a specific liaison officer is essential, as is the briefing of officers on the ground where housing enforcement teams may be operating. This officer should be informed of the execution of injunctions so as to facilitate the appropriate police response.

Facilitating the civil deterrent process. As detailed in the Gateshead case study, co-operation can be further operationalised by the local police issuing warning letters to tenants who precipitate police attendance for nuisance or criminal behaviour. Residents will be warned that they may be in breach of their tenancy agreement and the council have been informed of the incident.

Rather than the usual inter-agency discussion forum, such a partnership exchanges information according to daily operational requirements rather than at timetabled monthly meetings. The development of agency 'enforcement teams' and a corresponding police response can enable operational relationships to be established which utilise both the civil and criminal process.

Voids as crime magnets

Voids or empty properties have been called 'magnets for crime' and are well recognised as such by housing managers and police alike. They may facilitate criminal activity (drug and solvent abuse, storage of stolen goods) as well as being the target of it (theft, criminal damage, arson). The police service is clearly not responsible for the management of voids but an input to ameliorate the problem can be made. Commanders and patrol officers should be aware of the influence of voids, as precursors and targets of crime. Local officers should put pressure on the local authority to ensure the adequate securing of void properties. Similarly, with the increase in repossessions local officers should inform financial bodies of the risk faced by ill secured void properties.

Community based measures

In resolving local crime and nuisance behaviour the service must go beyond reacting to incidents to a problem solving approach, one consequence of which is establishing a partnership with the community. The philosophy of problem oriented policing (POP) is receiving increasing attention in the UK and sits well with the pro-active policing strategy promulgated by the Audit Commission, Home Office and HMIC. The working strategy of POP is well illustrated in the six concepts behind the Meadow Well Community Policing Unit (CPU) and the nine operational tactics adopted. This approach is detailed in the case study and will not be repeated here. The Meadow Well case study also epitomises the related themes of involving the community in looking for solutions as well as the shift in policing philosophy from reactive to pro-active.

Community relations

Residents must be seen as part of the solution and not the problem. It is important when discussing the variety of criminal and civil enforcement measures to remember that only a minority of residents on estates actually commit criminal offences or engage in anti-social behaviour. For any significant long term reductions the major resource in crime reduction, the community, must be harnessed. "A community must police itself. The police can, at best, only assist in that task." (Goldstein, 1990).

Opening up dialogue within 'closed' communities. It is common for an atmosphere of non-cooperation to be encountered in many high crime areas, such assistance being seen as 'grassing'. Two long term strategies to tackle the problem have been identified from the case studies. First, it must be recognised that despite the apparent prevalence of such hostility, many, if not the majority of residents, would be willing to co-operate with the police if their fear of intimidation was adequately addressed. Dealing with this problem may be accorded a higher priority if it is recognised that countering witness intimidation serves not only to aid investigation and prosecution, but also encourages wider police-community contact and communication. Secondly, with the possible exception of a hard core of individuals, many 'hostile' residents are not beyond reach and should not be discounted. It is only through non-confrontational contact that anti-police prejudices can be challenged. Neutral or positive interactions must be maximised to achieve this, a priority illustrated in the Meadow Well case study.

It should be noted, as an officer on the Meadow Well Estate commented, police officers may also hold negative preconceived opinions of residents which need similarly changing.

Communication, publicity and rumour control

Communication is necessary to engage residents, address fears and facilitate rumour control. One of the cornerstones in the effective policing of difficult housing estates is communication between the police and community bodies, individual officers and residents. There are two key objectives for such a communications strategy. First, in launching an anti-crime or community safety initiative, to encourage the support of residents and deter offenders. This was a clear priority for the Commander responsible for the Broxtowe Estate. Secondly, the police may need to engage, often rapidly and repeatedly, in rumour control following an incident. Significant investment in community relations can be lost on the basis of an incorrect rumour which takes hold. If an operation is considered potentially sensitive then the ground can be laid prior to implementation by explaining the need and benefits to the local community. If this is not possible for operational reasons, then a media strategy should be prepared beforehand and implemented immediately afterwards, in order to counter misinformation or mischievous rumours and reporting.

In addition to engaging with community groups, other means of reaching residents exist, such as:

- **local newspaper, TV and radio coverage.** Especially useful for special operations or problems which are more likely to attract media interest. Commanders (or their representatives) should be on first name terms with relevant broadcast and newspaper journalists.

- **a regular media slot.** It is increasingly common for local officers to provide a regular column in local newspapers which can also list police surgeries. Free newspapers are invariably receptive to such ideas. In the absence of existing local papers some force areas (eg Toxteth) have launched their own in partnership with other agencies and local businesses.

- **a phone-message service.** Easily established, permanently or temporarily. During the shooting incidents in Toxteth in the summer of 1995 a phone-line was installed, with a recorded message which provided a regular update on what had occurred and the status of the ongoing police investigation.

- **surgeries or police 'shops'.** Surgeries are often poorly attended because of their location. If an officer is sited amongst other community or local authority personnel then residents will pass through for other purposes and have a 'cover' if they choose to approach the officer. Toxteth has gone beyond this with a combined mini-station and community centre.

Developing a strategic approach

The variety of approaches to reducing crime and improving the quality of life on high crime housing estates and residential areas was discussed in the introduction to this report. A multitude of potential options exist. This report has confined itself to the initiatives which, directly or indirectly, involve the police service but even this presents local Commanders with an array of choices. On the basis of the examples discussed in this report, a successful strategy for tackling problem housing estates must include:

- action on three fronts: police, civil and community based measures.

- a combination of short and long term measures.

Table 7 illustrates these points with the initiatives discussed in the various case studies.

Table 7: A strategic approach to the policing of problem housing areas		
	Short term focus	Long term focus
Police measures	• Targeting offenders • Pro-active patrols • Pulse policing • Maximise visibility	• Intelligence gathering • Problem oriented policing • Counter witness intimidation
Civil measures	• Assist injunctions • Assist evictions	• Joint targeting of problems • Liaise with civil teams
Community measures	• Publicise initiatives • Rumour control • Leisure 'diversion' schemes	• Dialogue with the community • Generate positive contacts • Youth programmes* • Monitor void properties
Note: *Projects such as the Duke of Edinburgh Award Scheme and the longer term project in Toxteth are considered distinct from summer leisure schemes.		

The overall message is that the police cannot rely only on short term 'vigorous' policing to solve what have become in many cases almost intractable problems in an area. Neither can unrealistic expectations be placed on the shoulders of Community Beat Officers, residents' associations and similar bodies. What is required is action on all these fronts, combined in a strategic way to ensure an effective response to the problems presented by these particular housing estates. Vigorous enforcement activity from the police can make a significant impact, but these measures need to be followed up with work designed to consolidate such success into a more long term achievement.

Furthermore, the police are not the only agency capable of enforcement activity in problematic residential areas. The scope for civil instruments is broadening as their use by local authorities is successfully established. The police have a stake in these developments and Commanders need to be committed to investing the required resources where opportunities become present.

4. Conclusions and recommendations

This section summarises the good practice findings from the case studies. It is suggested that a successful policing strategy for tackling problem housing areas should involve police enforcement, civil actions and community based initiatives, in both short and long term activity, combined and co-ordinated in a strategic way.

Police enforcement

☞ All officers should be encouraged continuously to contribute to the gathering and logging of intelligence re offending and offenders on their estates.

☞ Special operations may be required to gather intelligence and evidence against key suspects.

☞ Significant problems may require a significant enforcement response such as high profile targeted patrols. Such operations should not be seen as incompatible with the objectives of community policing.

☞ Enforcement actions can be used to generate community support if targeted properly and accompanied by an explanation to residents using various media.

☞ Brief offence or area specific crackdowns at irregular intervals can be very effective at disrupting criminal activity.

☞ Measures, including appropriate performance indicators, should be introduced to maximise the visibility and frequency of regular foot patrols.

☞ Procedural measures to counter witness intimidation should be adopted as general policy. More resource intensive methods should be accorded a high priority where needed, to ensure the prosecution of offenders, to deter intimidation and to show residents that a commitment exists to tackle their problems.

Civil action

Commanders should:

☞ Be aware of the scope for local authorities to take civil action against nuisance and criminal local authority tenants.

☞ Encourage the local authority to take civil enforcement actions against those breaking tenancy agreements through criminal and nuisance behaviour. The use of specialist housing personnel can facilitate such actions, as can a review of tenancy agreements.

☞ Support civil actions by the provision of information to local authorities, where possible, and assist the operation of civil enforcement teams.

☞ Warn tenants that civil as well as criminal proceedings may follow incidents and disturbances attended by the police.

Community based measures

☞ The starting attitude of officers and Commanders should be that residents are part of the solution rather than the problem.

☞ Community relations and agency partnerships should be established to facilitate long term crime reduction initiatives, the objective of problem oriented policing. A more rigorous analysis of problems will help the development of this approach and the generation of innovative solutions.

☞ Opportunities should be created to increase the amount of positive, non-confrontational contact between police officers and residents.

☞ A better use of the media should be made to inform residents, address local fears, deter offenders and facilitate rumour control.

☞ The involvement of other agency personnel, such as housing staff, in obtaining witness statements should be encouraged.

☞ The police should encourage the adequate securing of void properties by local authorities and other financial bodies (eg banks).

References

Association of Metropolitan Authorities (1994) An unpublished survey and findings from an AMA seminar entitled 'Managing Neighbour Disputes, Nuisance and Crime on Council Estates; the Social Landlord', held in May 1994.

Department of the Environment (1993) *Crime Prevention on Council Estates.* London:HMSO.

Goddard, J. and Walker, J. (1993) *Evaluation of the Urban Crime Fund.* Centre for Research on Crime, Policing and the Community, Newcastle University.

Goldstein, H. (1990) *Problem-Oriented Policing.* New York: McGraw-Hill.

Mayhew, P., Aye Maung, N. and Mirrlees-Black, C. (1992) *The 1992 British Crime Survey.* Home Office Research Study 132. London:HMSO.

Maynard, W. (1994) *Witness Intimidation: Strategies for Prevention.* Police Research Group Crime Detection and Prevention Series Paper 55. London: Home Office.

Newman, O. (1972) *Defensible Space - Crime Prevention through Urban Design.* New York: Macmillan.

Sherman, L.W. (1990) Police Crackdowns: Initial and Residual Deterrence, *Crime and Justice: A Review of Research, Vol. 12* (Eds) Tonry, M. & Morris, N. Chicago: University of Chicago Press.

Appendix A

An example of a Beat Business Plan by a Beat Manager Constable in Killingbeck, Leeds

1) Vision

This part of the 'Beat Profile' asks what I would like my Community Beat to be like? Many words have been suggested to cover this area. Two certain words come to mind.

'Utopia' (Collins Dictionary Definition) - 'Any real or imaginary society, place, state etc considered to be perfect or ideal'

'Reality' (Collins Dictionary Definition) - 'The state of things as they are or appear to be rather than as one might wish them to be'

As can be seen by the above definitions, these two words seem to contradict one another. I believe working in any job including mine as a police officer, we have to be realistic when setting goals for achievement. The following statement is my 'Vision' for the community beat where I work,

> 'To assist in helping the residents of 16 beat to live their lives as they would want to, with as few distractions as is possible whether those distractions involve crime, nuisance or any other factor.'

2) Plan for 1994

This section deals with my specific objectives for the coming year. This year I will be looking at 2 specific areas of my long term aims.

1. Neighbourhood Watch Schemes

The Neighbourhood Watch schemes that I have inherited seem to have become a little run down. During the next seven months, I will be looking at the area and introducing more schemes and revitalising those current schemes which are already in existence. This will mean liaising with Crime Prevention Officers for up to date information and possibly, when they are established, inviting the CPOs to talk to the NHW schemes.

2. Council garages

During my time on this beat, it has come to light that when I give advice on vehicle crime, especially in the Stanks area, I come to the stumbling block that they have no where to put their vehicles other than on the road. On other occasions, information has come to light that the criminal fraternity are using some of the garages to hide motor vehicles that they have stolen so they can use them night after night or sell them on. I intend to approach the Housing Manager, Mr Bob Mooney with a view to reviewing this situation and with money permitting or finding council based schemes with finance available with a view to solving both problems at once. It may be advisable to target one set of the numerous garages in the area and use it as a pilot scheme to measure the success, if any.

Excerpts from the following section only are provided.

3) Objectives to be met - Long term strategy

Increasing Uniformed Patrols

The majority of my residents are from a good disciplined background and have grown up with good moral standards and have achieved a good financial status from their upbringing. They have an old fashioned idea of a police officer's role and still look for that in the modern day officer. Their confidence is given a boost by seeing a uniformed officer patrolling on foot in their particular street....I intend to keep this type of policing in the forefront of my aims as I feel it is an important part of my role.

Education

Many of the residents do not understand what a modern day police officer does within their area. I feel they need educating in this matter as well as being given objectives of their own in making their area a better place to live. Both objectives could be met with the introduction of more Neighbourhood Watch Schemes. I feel these schemes give the residents a feeling that they are contributing towards their own environments. It gives them an incentive to contribute rather than leaving it to other people. They also speak to myself on a regular basis. Getting to know me better may give them the confidence to pass on information about incidents in their area whereas on other occasions they may have been reluctant to call.

Youth

As mentioned earlier in the profile, many of the problems on the area are caused by males and females in the age group of 14-19 years. Tackling the youth problem becomes an important aspect of my role in the community.

In an effort to combat this area, I believe visits to local schools and youth organisations are very important, especially primary schools. These visits help me to build up relationships with these children and as a regular visitor they get to know me by my name and face. What is also important is that I also get to know names of these youths. I can gather information from teachers on known mischievous children and I can pay particular attention to these so if I meet them on the street, I have a good advantage over them by immediately knowing their name and what school they attend.

...I have a strong love for football and have used that to try to continue to build up our relationship. Along with my neighbouring beat manager, Pc 4170 Robinson, an annual small sided football tournament has been inaugurated with the schools and sponsorship from local firms and I hope in the future that this will continue.

Crime

Along with all the above mentioned aims, an important part of my role as a beat manager is to assist in reducing crime in my area. The above aims may in the future help in the long term to reduce the crime levels but there is an ongoing problem of the crimes committed on my beat. I feel my role in this matter is to try to be a good information gatherer for crime occurring on my beat. Getting to know the active criminals who reside on my beat and through patrolling the area, learning of changes to their appearance, vehicles they may be using, different addresses they may stay at, etc and passing this information on to other colleagues through the LIO system.

I also need to look at patterns of crime on my beat and instigate projects in an attempt to tackle these crime problems in their possible prevention and detection.

All the above aims are what I feel needs to be done on a year to year basis in an effort to move towards my vision of a better area for Beat 16.

Appendix B[3]

Civil legislative powers which may used by a local authority to tackle criminal or nuisance behaviour

The following is intended to give a broad indication of the scope of various powers, although it does not seek to be exhaustive. Relevant criminal powers held by the police, especially in regard to violence against the person and criminal damage have not been listed.

Local authority enabling powers

Subsidiary powers of local authorities

Section III of the Local Government Act 1972 gives local authorities the power to do anything (whether or not involving the expenditure, borrowing or lending of money or the acquisition or disposal of any property or rights) which is calculated to facilitate or is conducive or incidental to the discharge of any of their functions.

Powers of local authorities to prosecute or defend legal proceedings

Section 222 of the Local Government Act 1972

"Where a local authority considers it expedient for the promotion or protection of the interests of their area:

a) they may prosecute or defend or appear in any legal proceedings and in the case of civil proceedings, may institute them in their own name, and

b) they may in their own name make representations in the interests of the inhabitants at any public enquiry held by or on its behalf of any Minister or public body under any enactment."

General powers of management (housing)

Section 21 of the Housing Act 1985 gives general powers of management to local housing authorities to manage, regulate and control its housing stock. The general 'enabling' powers give local authorities considerable scope to develop and implement initiatives to enhance community safety, protect the community generally (particularly those most susceptible to the fear of crime and anti-social behaviour) and to take steps to support victims of such behaviour.

---

[3] This is an edited summary of legislative powers in Winning Communities (1994), published by the Association of District Councils.

Power of councils to make bye-laws for good rule and government and suppression of nuisance

Section 235 of the Local Government Act 1972 empowers local authorities to make bye-laws for good rule and government and suppression of nuisance.

Bye-laws (housing)

Section 23 of the Housing Act 1985 enables local housing authorities to make bye-laws for the management, use and regulation of their houses.

Powers of entry

Section 16 Environmental Protection Act.

Section 17 Environmental Protection Act.

Public Health (Control of Diseases) Act 1984.

Use of property for illegal activity

Powers to deprive offender of property used or intended to be used for purpose of crime - Section 43 of the Powers of Criminal Courts Act 1973.

Tenant permitting premises to be used as a brothel or for prostitution - Sections 35 and 36 of the Sexual Offences Act 1956.

Intimidation or annoyance by violence or otherwise

Violence for securing entry - Section 6 Criminal Law Act 1977.

Adverse occupation of residential premises - Section 7 Criminal Law Act 1977.

Trespassing with a weapon of offence - Section 8 Criminal Law Act 1977.

Other - Section 7 Conspiring and Protection of Property Act 1875.

Malicious phone calls - Telecommunication Act 1954.

Protection of public rights (highways)

Section 130 of the Highways Act 1980 places a duty on a highway authority to assert and protect the rights of the public to the use and enjoyment of any highway including any roadside waste which forms part of it.

Compensation orders against convicted persons - Section 35 of the Powers of Criminal Courts Act 1973.

Race relations

Section 71 of the Race Relations Act 1976 places a duty on every local authority to make appropriate arrangements with a view to securing that their various functions are carried out with due regard to the need:

a)   to eliminate unlawful racial discrimination, and

b)   to promote equality of opportunity and good relations, between persons of different racial groups.

Local authorities should also have regard to the Commission for Racial Equality statutory Codes of practice - 'Code of Practice in Rented Housing' and 'Code of Practice for the elimination of Racial Discrimination and promotion of Equal Opportunity in Employment'.

Part 1 of the Public Order Act sets out a range of relevant offences regarding abusive language and physical attack.

Removal from property

Prosecution of offences (Eviction)

Section 6 Protection from Eviction Act 1977 empowers local authorities to institute proceedings for an offence under this Act.

Squatting

Order 113 Rules of the Supreme Court and Order 24 Part 1 County Court Rules

Vehicles and parking

Street repair of vehicles - Town Police Clauses Act 1847.

Abandoned vehicles - Refuse Disposal (Amenity) Act 1978 Local Authorities.

Parking on verges or pavements - Motor Vehicle Regulations Act 1986.

Illegal parking of vehicles - Sections 19, 21, 22 Road Traffic Act 1988.

Prohibition of driving motor vehicles elsewhere than on roads - Section 34 Road Traffic Act 1988.

Vacant derelict, neglected land and unoccupied buildings

Planning Policy Guidance PPG3 Housing can be used to eliminate sites which are often the focus of a range of anti-social activities such as fly tipping, abandoned vehicles, rubbish, and may provide a focus for criminal activities etc.

Local authorities may undertake any works necessary to prevent unauthorised entry, or prevent buildings becoming a danger to public health, on any building which is unoccupied or where the occupier is temporarily absent, and which is not effectively secured against unauthorised entry or likely to become a danger to public health.

Refuse and litter

Removal of noxious matter - Section 79 Public Health Act 1936.

Accumulations of rubbish - Sections 34 and 283 Public Health Act 1936.

Abandoned trolleys - Section 99 and Schedule 4 Environmental Protection Act 1990.

Statutory nuisances

Section 79 of the Environmental Protection Act 1990 lists various nuisances or factors prejudicial to health including animals, noise, smell, smoke or any accumulation or deposit.

See also:

Control of Pollution (Special Waste) Regulations 1980.

Section 87 Environmental Protection Act 1990.

Litter (Animal Droppings) Order and Part IV Environmental Protection Act 1990.

RECENT POLICE RESEARCH GROUP CRIME DETECTION AND PREVENTION SERIES PAPERS:

58. **Combating Burglary: An Evaluation of Three Strategies.** Janet Stockdale and Peter Gresham. 1995.

59. **Biting Back: Tackling Repeat Burglary and Car Crime.** David Anderson, Sylvia Chenery and Ken Pease. 1995.

60. **Policing and Neighbourhood Watch: Strategic Issues.** Gloria Laycock and Nick Tilley. 1995.

61. **Investigating, Seizing and Confiscating the Proceeds of Crime.** Michael Levi and Lisa Osofsky. 1995.

62. **Performance Indicators for Local Anti-Drugs Strategies – A Preliminary Analysis.** Mike Chatterton, Christine Godfrey, Gwendy Gibson, Mark Gilman, Matthew Sutton and Alan Wright. 1995.

63. **Preventing School Bullying.** John Pitts and Philip Smith. 1995.

64. **Intelligence, Surveillance and Informants: Integrated Approaches.** Mike Maguire and Timothy John. 1995.

65. **Local Crime Analysis.** Tim Read and Dick Oldfield. 1995.

66. **The Nature and Extent of Heavy Goods Vehicle Theft.** Rick Brown. 1995.

67. **Reducing Repeat Racial Victimisation on an East London Estate.** Alice Sampson and Coretta Phillips. 1995.

68. **Closed Circuit Television in Town Centres: Three Case Studies.** Ben Brown. 1995.

69. **Disrupting the Distribution of Stolen Electrical Goods.** Egmont Kock, Tim Kemp and Bernard Rix. 1995.

70. **Crime Risk Management: Making it work.** Cressida Bridgeman. 1996.

71. **Tackling Car Crime. An Evaluation of Sold Secure.** Rick Brown & Nicola Billing. 1996

72. **Methadone Maintenance and Crime Reduction on Merseyside.** Howard Parket & Perpetua Kirby. 1996.

73. **Forensic Science and Crime Investigation.** Adrian Leigh, Tim Read & Nick Tilley. 1996.